WEAPONS
OF
MASS DISTRACTION

Dismantling the Influence
of
Negative Hip-Hop Music
on Our Youth

written by

Hayward R. Jean

edited by
Terry R. Cortese, MFA

Editing and Book Layout by Terry Cortese, New Learning Concepts, Inc. Bloomington, Indiana.

Cover Design by Greg Jackson, Thinkpen Design, Springdale, Arkansas

Library of Congress Control Number: 2018913073

ISBN 9780692043066

In Loving Memory

I am grateful to the Matriarch of our family, my grandmother, Rosa Quiller Butler. The love of music she instilled in my family will live on throughout eternity. This project is connected to the legacy of my grandmother and her love for people. I carry this legacy with dignity and determination.

Contents

About the Author

Born and raised in Langley, South Carolina, Hayward Renel Jean is the son of Vanessa Butler of Langley, South Carolina and Raynold Jean of Haiti. He was raised with his twin brother and younger sister. Jean (pronounced "John") is the principal of Mellichamp Elementary School in Orangeburg, South Carolina.

At Mellichamp Elementary School, Hayward and his dynamic team of professionals are making history. Together they were one of eight South Carolina schools in 2013 to go from an "F" rating to an "A" rating in one year. This school consistently meets standard towards the 2020 SC Performance Vision, and in 2014, they were the recipient of the school's first ever Palmetto Silver Award for academic performance. Today Mellichamp is continuing to empower students to accomplish greatness by helping students maximize potential. The school has a ballet studio to discover professional dancers, a chess club and a tennis club, a golf mentoring program, an entrepreneur club, Step teams, the Gentlemen's club, and Girls club, a STEM club and a public speaking club. These are designed to educate the whole child and to develop leadership skills within the youth.

Hayward is a member of the inaugural class of the nationally acclaimed Call Me MISTER program. In 2001 Jean, was seen on the Oprah Winfrey Show with Call Me MISTER leaders during the show's "Use Your Life Award" segment. Also featured during that episode was award-winning playwright and actor, Tyler Perry.

As an educator, Hayward has been featured in *The Wall Street Journal*, *Education Week*, a Center for American Progress executive summary, *The Times* and *Democrat* newspapers, where he was named as one of the top ten citizens who made a difference in Orangeburg, SC, and the ETV documentary entitled, *Call Me MISTER*.

The South Carolina NAACP awarded Hayward the Presidential Citation Award for Education Advocacy in 2009. National education expert, Salome Thomas-EL writes of Jean in his award-winning book entitled, *The Immortality of Influence*, with a foreword written by actor, Will Smith. Hayward is also featured on the front cover of the book entitled, *Call Me MISTER: The Re-emergence of African American Male Teachers*, written by Dr. Roy Jones, executive director of Call Me MISTER, and oral historian, Aretta Jenkins. Hayward was honored as Claflin University's first Young Alumnus Visionary Award recipient featured in the University's Hall of Fame and is a member of the Orangeburg Young Professionals' 20 executives under 40. Recently, Hayward was featured on the cover of ASCD's leadership brochure.

In addition to serving as an educator, Hayward also serves as the assistant pastor of The Feast of the Lord in Orangeburg, SC. He is also a songwriter with a featured song on award-winning gospel projects of which he tells of his story growing up without his biological father in the song, "Still, My Father." As a motivational speaker Hayward is the founder of Speak Life Enterprises. He is happily married to the phenomenal Mrs. Starlette Jean. They have three children, Hayward, Malachi, and Imani.

From the Author

As a principal of an elementary school, I've heard students say some of the most shocking statements. But, none of the statements top the one I heard from a fifth grader. For the sake of privacy, we'll call this fifth grader Justin. It was a normal day after school as Justin, his friends, and I sat in the cafeteria. As the students sat chatting, I monitored the cafeteria. My attention was drawn to Justin and his friends when I overheard them talking about a rap battle. I smiled and thought back to my younger days when my friends and I used to battle rap against each other. My memories brought forth laughter as I walked closer and told the boys I wanted to get in on the fun. They snickered and said, "Mr. Jean?!" in a shocking tone. I laughed back and said, "Hey, don't let the suit fool you!"

They continued in their rap battle going back and forth with one another. The rest of them sat laughing and enjoying the show, but my laughter quickly turned into frustration when I heard some of Justin's lyrics, which were from a popular hip-hop song about killing and drugs. This wasn't the content my friends and I used to rap battle. Out of nowhere, this 11-year-old boy was speaking the most grotesque, sexual language you can think of. It took me no time to break up their fun.

I was flustered, aggravated and appalled. In less than 30 seconds, Justin had rapped about killing people, gang activity, and foul sexual remarks. Yet, he didn't even have a clue of the obscenity that had come from his mouth! "It's just music," he said. Even worse, Justin was one of my students who struggled academically. Yet he was able to recite a whole song by Jay Z. I would love for mainstream hip-hop artists to understand that what they are putting out to the masses is having a negative effect on young people. I believe they too are distracted by the fame and fortune that comes with their careers. While I hope to influence and inspire today's artists to improve the content of their work in such a way that would help our youth, my major focus is helping our youth to choose life by helping them to focus on fulfilling their destinies.

That's right—I said choose life! I want our kids to choose life and speak life, not death. If Justin had known the words coming out his mouth were about killing, gangs, and bloodshed, I think he may have better understood what I was trying to say when I pulled him aside that afternoon and explained to him how deadly his lyrics were.

Maybe Justin didn't understand what I meant when I called his music deadly. After all, to him, his friends, and the rest of the hip-hop and pop music industry it's "just music." Maybe Justin will look back one day and remember my advice. Perhaps, ten, twenty or thirty years from now, that moment and my words will come back to him and spark a movement. But, even if Justin never remembers the words I told him, I hope he has a chance to pick up this book.

Weapons of Mass Distraction is the first part of my literary movement to give tools to our youth and those who love them to combat the evil forces steering them away from their path to a purposeful life. Through this book, the youth and those who love them will discover their true value and will not forfeit or abort their destinies with destructive words and images put to rhythm and rhyme. *Weapons of Mass Distraction* calls every reader to rise to a new level of thinking when it comes to what one allows inside of one's mind and spirit. The challenges and distractions I had to overcome to produce this work are confirmation that this is written for some extraordinary people. After reading this book, your life will never be the same and hopefully Justin, and the young people like him, will change their mindsets too.

Introduction:
What Are Weapons of Mass Distraction?

The year was 2010. It was a normal day with one of my mentees on the basketball court. I had several mentees at the time, but this one was different. His name was Jaquez. He was a smart, athletic teenager who was about to enter the ninth grade. Despite his intelligence, his run-ins with the law left him with a lengthy record of crime, violence and petty theft. Oddly enough, his personality and attire never fit in with the gangster lifestyle he tried to emulate. Anybody could look at him in a crowd of thugs and easily tell he didn't fit in. He wore Dockers, a polo shirt, and could speak articulately about the first world war. Yet, he had begun to mimic the behaviors described in the lyrics he listened to.

Jaquez was distracted. He was distracted by girls, stacks of money, and video games. Unfortunately, the words in his music encouraged his distractions. Jaquez grew up without a father, so the only male role models in his life were 50 Cent, Lil' Wayne, Waka Flocka Flame, and his older brother, Phillip who at the time was facing a life sentence for murder.

While many said Jaquez was destined for the worst, I disagreed, that's why I spent so many days trying to mentor him through the game of basketball.

"Look Jaquez," I sternly told him one day after one of our basketball games.

"You've got to aim in life the same way you aim at that hoop. Think of this ball as your energy and that net as your destiny. When you're shooting, you aren't looking at the distractions around you. You're focused on the one goal in front of you and that is where you aim your energy. Life can be the same way."

"Yeah, yeah, I know man, but it's hard to stay focused out here," he responded as he looked down at the hot, beat up pavement on the basketball court.

I spent a lot of time mentoring Jaquez because, despite his surroundings, upbringing, and older brother, I knew his possibilities were greater than his current circumstances. Whenever he wasn't in the detention center, Jaquez was known for making all A's in school. His destiny didn't have to be like his present if he could just learn to stop being so distracted.

My childhood was a lot like Jaquez's upbringing, which is probably one of the reasons I spent so much time with him. My father wasn't around growing up and much of my neighborhood was poor and permeated with drugs and petty crime, too. The fact that I sometimes sneaked around behind my Mom's back to listen to Cam'ron who rapped about everything from sex to violence didn't help. Nevertheless my mother, relentless in speaking inspirational words into my life, helped me to strive for greater than the expectations of my impoverished environment. I pushed past the odds by learning to get away from my distractions. Then, I began to replace the filthy words of death with words of life. I became so fascinated with my purpose that I developed a passion for helping others to find and fulfill theirs. So, from firsthand experience, I knew Jaquez's problem didn't stem from his innate abilities or tendencies, but rather from his distractions.

If I could just teach Jaquez to keep his eye on his aspirations the way I had taught him to keep his eye on the rim! I wanted him to soar higher than I did and do greater than I had done. And, I knew the only way he could do that would be for me to put words in his life that would speak to his destiny and not his demise. That was what saved me, so I knew it could save him too. Sadly, there seemed to be a mental block that often kept my advice from influencing him. When I spoke to him about his negative decisions, he never seemed to hear. Like many young teens, he seemed to think that if Lil' Wayne smoked weed, he should do it too.

It was clear. His future was full of potential. But his distraction, his music, was louder than the call to live up to his fullest potential. His music wasn't just a distraction—it was a massive distraction. A massive distraction that acted as a weapon, slowly but surely, driving him, his friends, and anyone else distracted by the music, away from their life's purpose. Although I recognized the potential in him, Jaquez wasn't convinced of his own greatness.

One Saturday afternoon, following one of our basketball games, Jaquez confided in me that he wasn't happy with who he was. Kids were bullying him and he had been getting into more fights in school. He was depressed, smoking more marijuana, and his anger towards his parents and teachers had increased. He didn't know how to deal with his depression and he felt like life was becoming too much for him to bear. He didn't want the life he was living anymore—the fighting, the jail, and the violence. But he didn't know a way out. For him his only escape was his music. Sadly, he didn't realize that his music wasn't enabling him to escape his problems, but rather to become more enslaved by them. I, along with so many others, assured him that if he continued to focus on school, and tune out his distractions, everything would be alright. Unfortunately, he did not heed my advice. That afternoon was the last time I saw Jaquez. Due to various circumstances, time passed and we lost touch. Months later, I found out he had shot himself.

****

Since our youth only hear music that talks about killing and drug-dealing, when a child loses a fight in life the only alternative he has heard of is death. The music provides no other choices. This is referenced in much of the culture of gangster music, which tells listeners to "Get Rich or Die Trying." In Jaquez's case, his musical influences, while not the reason for his death, provided only false hopes and didn't give him the tools needed to combat the temptations that ultimately led to his demise.

Just like Jaquez, suicidal thoughts often came to me in my youth. But, at an early age I was introduced to my true identity. The more I understood that my life had meaning, the more I realized how meaningless lyrics could cause me to devalue the greatness I possessed. Although Jaquez's music didn't help him, it is not what killed him. His circumstances didn't kill him either. Jaquez's real problem wasn't just that he had negative influences; it was that he didn't have anything to hold on to. As a kid going in and out jail and growing up without a father, he had very little he could count on. So, he latched on to what was most familiar to him, his music. He couldn't see his all "A" report cards, or the amazing potential he possessed beyond all his distractions. And, when life became too difficult, his favorite songs did not sustain him.

In times of trouble, 50 Cent's lyrics couldn't keep Jaquez going. He needed something much greater to keep him in that dark time in his life. He needed to know that things were going to get better. But his music, the lyrics that encouraged him to continue living the life he was living, kept speaking louder than the other encouraging voices around him. Whenever I, a teacher, or another mentor in Jaquez's life tried to talk some sense into him, he almost always used a lyric from one of his rap idols to defend himself. Yet, in times of despair, those same lyrics held nothing for him. In Jaquez's life, the voices of encouragement couldn't speak as loud as the voices of his music. His music had influenced him to continue to be promiscuous, to steal and to engage in drug activity, but it couldn't influence him to protect his own life. When our kids hear nothing but killing in their music, what is going to be there to sustain them when those lyrics become a reality? Who will give them hope when the distractions become too much to bear?

The problem is that this music is influencing our children to assume identities that are inappropriate and even detrimental to them. Giving attention to racy songs about drugs, illegal money-making schemes and gang affiliations is distracting to young people who are already faced with enough challenges—trying find out who they are and why they exist.

Mainstream hip-hop is a component of a culture that dominates massive groups of elementary, middle, high school and college-aged students' attitudes and behaviors, particularly males. As an elementary school principal, I noticed the same kids I'd reprimanded for singing the lyrics to "Hot N---a," by Bobby Shmurda were the kids that were sent to my office for extreme misbehavior. The lyrics in that song are as follows:

> Run up on that n---a get to squeezing, hoe,
> Everybody catching bullet holes,
> N----s got me on my bully yo,
> I'm a run up, put that gun on 'em,

I'm a run up, go dumb on 'em.

Appropriately, the artist of that song, Bobby Shmurda, coined the last name of his stage name by putting the words "sh" and "murder" together, symbolizing his support for the "no snitching" movement as it pertains to crimes such as murder. Many people add "sh" to a word when they want to devalue, show sarcasm or belittle the meaning of an item or idea. "Sh"murda, with his lyrics attempts to minimize the impact that taking another human's life has on our world.

While Shmurda remains quiet and nonchalant about murder, his deathly lyrics scream loud in the hearts and minds of our youth. I see this particularly in the groups of males who love his music and believe fighting is the answer. So often, students suspended for fighting, aren't just the same youth who mimic the music of hip-hop artists, but they are also the same children I later see in the newspaper headlines for murder, assault, and serious drug offenses.

Our inner-city youth who grow up without role models, often look to these artists as mentors. Every day youth like Jaquez who follow the culture of hip-hop music also begin to follow its lifestyle. Yes—lifestyle! The lyrics of violence, crime, and drugs aren't just words chanted to a beat, they often represent the reality of the everyday lives of citizens struggling to live in impoverished and tense environments. On an annual basis, more hip-hop and rap artists are incarcerated than artists in any other genre of music. Once released from prison, many rappers rap about being locked up as if it is a badge of honor. In fact, there are many rap songs that were either written or recorded in jail cells. Drug and crime infested music aren't leading our youth to their future, but they are leading them to untimely funerals.

Every time an inappropriate rap song is recorded and released to the masses, it contains a message that has the potential to teach and train youth in the ways of violence and crime. There are even songs that are intentional about teaching youth the wrong way, as indicated by their titles alone. One song that's a great example of this is, "Oh, Let's Do It," by Georgia rapper, Waka Flocka Flame. As a former teacher, I once heard an eight-year-old child rapping this song as he sang the lyrics:

> I f----d my money up, now I can't re-up, run up in his spot, just to get my stacks up, now I'm back on deck, so shawty what the f--k you want, N----s talkin' s--t, but this ain't what the f--k he want, locked my CEO up, now it's back to coka, N----s talkin' s---t bruh, hang him by the ropa, hit 'em with the choppa, call that s--t hot lava, call me Waka Flocka aka young wild N---a, aka young drug dealer…Yeah, O let's do it….drug dealin' music…I influence…I influence (Malphurs, 2009).

In this song, Waka Flocka is stating that his solution to his money problems is either armed robbery or selling cocaine. His lyrics are filled with romanticized musings about drugs, violence, and killing. As that eight-year-old rapped, I noticed that he paused in silence between every other word in the song. When I approached the eight-year-old, I asked him why he paused so frequently in the song. I'll never forget his response.

"Those are curse words!" he answered in a high-pitched voice.

To the boy, intentionally eliminating the curse words out of the song made the song clean. But, the real obscenity of the song wasn't the swearwords. Rather, it was the meaning of the words that remained. This child blatantly talked about killing "n----s" with bullets, infesting neighborhoods with drugs, and other violent behavior. But he didn't notice anything obscene in the song until he came to the profanity! Our youth, radio stations, and music producers must understand that a song cannot be clean when it pollutes the minds of the people who listen to it.

A State of Emergency

It's clear that as a society we are in a state of emergency. I first began referring to mainstream hip-hop music as weapons of mass distraction on September 11, 2001. At the time, the term "Weapons of Mass Destruction" became famous in popular culture because of the senseless World Trade Center terrorist attacks. President George W. Bush used the term, weapons of mass destruction, because the attacks of September 11th led special intelligences to discover that there were possible weapons that needed to be found and confiscated in Iraq. As I pondered this term one day, I realized mainstream hip-hop music is just like a terrorist attack designed to take out as many young people as possible in the time it takes to listen to a song. There are musical weapons destroying our youth, neighborhoods and school systems. While I was in great sorrow for the lives of the 911 victims and their families, overtime I became equally sensitive to the lives of thousands of youth with aborted destinies and to the conflicted musical messages that were a part of their daily lives.

Because of negative rap music's power to move a massive amount of people, it is in fact not just a weapon of mass destruction, but also a Weapon of Mass Distraction. The destructive content and energy of these songs is not designed to kill the listeners, but to move them away from who they are and to distract them from their life's purpose, just like it did for

Jaquez. A weapon of mass distraction moves its listener away from where he should be, taking his focus off the intended, prioritized and appropriate goals. This leaves the listener still breathing, but under the influence of the negative music. The youth who listens to this music is also left with the potential to negatively influence others as they have been influenced.

Even 50 Cent himself called his third album *The Massacre* as 1.14 million people bought his album in one week. The album sold 13 million copies worldwide. That's 13 million plus people listening to "Candy Shop," one of the chart-topping singles in the album, which happens to be a song about oral sex. I think "massacre" is the right term for what took place metaphorically with the selling of that album and the impact on young minds—a mental massacre. While the content of "Candy Shop" is a metaphor for intense sexual activity, the literal content, candy, is attractive and a strong distraction for young minds. Images in past songs such as: Nicki Minaj's "Barbie," Rihanna's "Birthday Cake," Keli's "Milkshake," Soulja Boy's "Superman," and a host of others follow this pattern of using playful childhood items or characters as symbols of various sex acts or sexual images. This is particularly dangerous territory as it risks confusing both children and adults about how to treat sex and sexual partners.

Am I saying that 50 Cent, Lil Wayne, and Waka Flocka Flame killed Jaquez? No. Did their songs kill the eight-year-old who loved to rap Waka Flocka's songs as he waited for his mom at the bus stop? No. My principle concern isn't that this music is killing or abusing our kids. My major concern is that it's distracting them. It's moving them closer to a life of short-term rewards and further away from a path that leads toward success in school and in life. When our youth become the music they listen to, the artists win sales and the youth lose themselves.

When our youth become engrossed in the influences of their music, it's difficult for anything or anyone else to penetrate their minds. Just like that memorable Saturday afternoon when I told Jaquez "not to give up," and he refused my advice, our kids are shutting their ears to the positive influences in their lives, while something much louder is screaming through their headphones.

When lyrics about violence and fighting deter a child from affirming life, the only direction he can turn toward is death. If music moves our youth and nothing else positive can get through to give them hope, what will be there to sustain them?

Words are seeds. Seeds are meant to be planted to grow. Words have creative power. Jaquez chose to embody the lyrics of the music he listened to. His suicide happened long before he turned the gun on himself. The poison in much of mainstream hip-hop music is causing our youth to commit spiritual suicide. They come to believe the life they were given isn't worth living and they become someone else right before our eyes.

To Educators...
from an Educator

Chapter One:
Live Fast, Die Young?

...Die young but f--k it, we flew first class
Turned you to a rich b---h buy you first class
Up in this b---h and we lit up the screen
Every time we hit the charts n----s shoot up like
a fiend
Stuntin' like we printin' money wit' machines...
[Chorus]
They say we can't be livin' like this for the rest of
our lives
Well we gon' be livin' like this for the rest of
tonight
And you know they gon' be bangin' this s--t for
the rest of our lives
So live fast and die young, live fast and die young,
live fast and die young...

These lyrics represent the underlying theme of much of today's mainstream hip-hop music. The above lyrics by William Leonard Roberts II (better known by his stage name Rick Ross), are from his popular song entitled "Live Fast, Die Young," featuring Kanye West. The song implies that the artist has been advised not to live life so carelessly. Although the artist understands the advice, he decides to make the most out of the night with the expectation not to live a long life. Roberts, a.k.a. Rick Ross, derived his stage name from a well-known illegal drug trafficker named Ricky Donnell Ross. With songs like these playing repeatedly on the radio, young people are offered the opportunity to give up on their dreams for the temporary satisfactions that come from money and sex.

Rick Ross has often been compared to the late, well-known rapper, Christopher Wallace, better known by his stage name Biggie Smalls, a.k.a. Notorious B.I.G. Biggie Smalls, who died of multiple gunshot wounds in 1997. While he was alive, he recorded many songs that contained much of today's similar content about drugs, sex and murder. His first album, *Ready to Die*, became certified platinum four times, which means masses of people purchased the album. This album contained songs such as: "Gimme the Loot," "Ready to Die," "One More Chance," "Juicy," and the extremely popular, "Suicidal Thoughts." Since the album is entitled *Ready to Die*, one can't help but wonder, was the rapper trying to send a message when he recorded the song, "Suicidal Thoughts"? The lyrics are as follows:

> When I die, f--k it I wanna go to hell
> Cause I'm a piece of s--t, it ain't hard to f----n' tell
> It don't make sense, goin' to heaven with the goodie-goodies
> Dressed in white, I like black Tims and black hoodies...
> ...All my life I been considered as the worst
> Lyin' to my mother, even stealin' out her purse
> Crime after crime, from drugs to extortion
> I know my mother wished she got a f----g abortion
> She don't even love me like she did when I was younger
> Suckin' on her chest just to stop my f----n' hunger
> I wonder if I died, would tears come to her eyes
> Forgive me for my disrespect, forgive me for my lies

My baby mother's eight months, her little sister's
two
Who's to blame for both of them, (naw n---a, not
you)
I swear to God I just want to slit my wrists and
end this bulls--t
Throw the Magnum to my head, threaten to pull
s--t
And squeeze, until the bed's completely red
I'm glad I'm dead, a worthless f----n' buddah head
The stress is building up, I can't
I can't believe suicide's on my f-----g mind, I
wanna leave
I swear to God I feel like death is f-----g calling
me
Naw you wouldn't understand (N---a, talk to me
please)
...Call my n---a Chic, tell him that my will is
weak
I'm sick of n----s lying, I'm sick of b-----s hawkin'
Matter of fact, I'm sick of talkin' [sound of a
gunshot].

Biggie Smalls' second and final album, *Life After Death*
was released fifteen days after he died. Why would one of the
most successful and wealthiest rappers write a song as graphic as
"Suicidal Thoughts"? In an interview recorded in the *New York
Times*, Biggie Smalls states, "One thing I learned about the game
is when you get a lot of money, n-----s don't like you. I'm getting
more money now.... I'm not paranoid to the point where... Yes, I
am. I'm scared to death. Scared of getting my brains blown out"

(*The New York Times*, December 18, 1994). After gleaning this information from the legend of hip-hop himself, how can anyone possibly dismiss his art as "just music?" These lyrics sound like a cry for help and, to me, clearly reflect that Biggie Smalls needed a counselor more than he needed a concert.

Biggie Smalls had little opportunity to enjoy his childhood. As his recent biopic and several autobiographical sources reveal, he began selling crack cocaine as early as 12 years old. "My customers were ringing my bell, and they would come up on the steps and smoke right here. They knew where I lived; they knew my moms" (*The New York Times*). "I heard about crack on the news and I was like, 'That's what n----s must be doing,'" Wallace recalled in an interview.

As a child, Biggie Smalls was exposed to and participated in self-destructive activity with a legacy of gangster rap music left behind. Many of today's youth, who may never sell drugs or join gangs, are invited to this type of life through the lyrical content of rappers that rap out their pain. After much research, I am convinced that The Notorious B.I.G. needed, and many other rappers need, as much mentorship and guidance as many of their listeners do.

Tupac Shakur

Another one of mainstream hip-hop music's legends, the late Tupac Shakur, speaks of dying young in his song "Death Around the Corner." In the song he raps,

> My homie told me once
> Don't you trust them other suckers
> They fought like they your homies
> But they phony motherf-----s
> And even if I did die young, who cares

All I ever got was mean mugs and cold stares
I got homies in my head who done passed away
screaming
please Young n---a, make Gs
I can't give up, although I'm hopeless
I think my mind's gone
All I can do is get my grind on, death around the
corner...

This does not sound like someone that wants fans, but someone in need of friends...true friends. He goes on to rap:

I was raised in the city, sh---y
Ever since I was an itty bitty kitty
Drinkin' liquor out my momma's t--ty
And smokin' weed was an everyday thing in my
household
And drinking liquor 'til you out cold
And tho' I'm gone now, n----a it's still on—
Pow, Busting on them n----s 'til they gone
How many more jealous a-- b-----s,
coming for my riches
Now I gotta stay suspicious...

On September 7, 1996, Shakur was fatally shot in a drive-by shooting in Las Vegas, Nevada. He was taken to the University Medical Center of Southern Nevada where he died six days later. I can still hear Tupac's music playing in the streets today and see young people not even born at the time of Tupac's death wearing t-shirts bearing his face.

The Bomb Beats

How could songs about suicide, dying young and death being around the corner be considered entertainment? If you take all vocals off the three tracks mentioned, you would only have some very catchy and heart pounding instrumental beats! Many times, artists do not have words to songs until they hear beats, which proves that even the rappers themselves are drawn to the beats. This could be naive, but I don't believe that many of our youth, and the adults who love them, actually agree with the content in much of rap music. However, I do believe they are massively distracted by the beats of the songs that cause them to listen to music they would probably detest if the beats weren't "the bomb!" "The bomb" is right because the beats have the power to move so many of our youth away from life and toward self-destruction. How else could one nod his or her head to a song about a man's suicidal thoughts? We must come to realize that no beat is good enough to allow self-destructive information to be injected over and over again into the minds of our youth. The chorus repeats the destructive content, reinforcing its negative message. There is a force that is a factor in all of this, and this force has an objective to steal, kill, and destroy people. Weapons of Mass Distraction steal, kill, and destroy people's lives by placing limits on their abilities to do what they have been created to do. One of my good friends, a very successful artist and lyricist Glover Richberg says, "Don't forget to use your own minds." I want to empower the youth and those who love them to use their own minds. Don't let the musical beats put you in a trance and take you away to a place of entertainment without considering what it is you're being entertained by.

Our youth have so much to live for. To live fast and die young constitutes a lifestyle of selfishness, illegality, violence and ultimate self-destruction. Weapons of Mass Distraction go beyond making money to a place that ensures the listeners do not make the money or experience the success of the artists. It is interesting that artists tell fans to die young, while they are moving about with security guards, in private planes living in huge mansions and earning enough money to afford proper health care. Many consumers of this music that I spend time with daily as an educator, are in poverty. The attractiveness of the artists' lifestyle mixed with the bomb beats are so distracting to our young people that they know the lyrics to gangster rap songs better than they know how to read and write. The competing interests of this type of entertainment kill our youth's ability to think for themselves. My sentiments are that of positive Grammy award-winning rapper, Lecrae, that raps in his song, "Nuthin'": "I know they gon' label me a hater/But inside they are greater than the songs they creatin'…" In this song Lecrae, with his amazing beats and phenomenal flow, raps about the influence of mainstream hip-hop music and how it is indeed having an adverse effect on the youth. Lecrae continues:

> It's little homies in the hood regurgitating
> And everybody watching thinking that you made it
> The truth is for a few designer labels and a little
> bit of paper now you 12 years slaving
> Hey but you ain't Lupita
> So why you beat up
> and pushing people to lean on the double cup and
> a seizure
> It sound like you put your feet up
> You still a slave and money can't buy you
> freedom partna'…"

Mainstream hip-hop artists can be great without Weapons of Mass Distraction. I love the fact they are talented, confident and have overcome some difficult circumstances, but to turn their stories into positive influences for the youth, they must tell their fans there is no happy ending to the lifestyles they describe in their music. The truth must be told! Lecrae goes on to rap,

> And every song talking 'bout they selling work on every corner
> Don't talk about the laws, taking kids away from mommas
> Don't talk about your homie in the trauma cause he shot up
> Or what about your young boy messing up the product
> They don't talk about the bond money that they ain't have
> And everybody snitch on everybody in the jam
> They don't talk about the pain, they don't talk about the struggle
> How they turn to the Lord when they ran into trouble.
> I'm a talk about it
> I don't care if the world try to swallow me
> I turn my back to 'em, tell 'em all follow me...
> [Outro:] Hey man, the way I see it, I think we were made for more than just, ya know, the simple things that we aspire toward. We were made for more than just telling stories about how much money we can get by selling poison to people. It's time to talk about who we are and who we can be. And we need to build each other up and not put

each other down. I feel like we not talking about nothing right now.)

I appreciate Lecrae for being an example of coming through some of the same lifestyles that most of the mainstream hip-hop artists endured. As gifted as he is, he too could rap just as well or better than most about the "same old" stuff (i.e. girls, cars, money, cribs, watches, etc.). Instead, he realized there is no happy ending to the love of money, and once he got to a place of restoration, he reached back to influence the masses to take their lives in a positive direction.

Rick Ross and Kanye West mention Biggie Smalls and Tupac in the song, "Live Fast and Die Young." I do not believe this is a coincidence because they both rapped about living fast and, sadly, both men died young. The Notorious B.I.G. died at age 24 and Tupac Amaru Shakur died at age 25. They were in the same age group as many of the young men and women I mentor today. Most of the songs they left behind, and their tragic, untimely and unfortunate deaths certainly support the notion of living fast and dying young. And even after their death our youth are still distracted by their music.

Teaching and learning for students of today must blend educational content with what is needed to live a productive and inspiring life of service to mankind. Real-world and personalized learning are critical to reaching our youth. If we don't make the effort to reach them, other meaningless alternatives will.

Chapter Two:
Speak Life!

Our spirit is the real life in us, and who better to speak on the power of music than one of the singers who has made an impact on this world with his musical gift. Award-winning Gospel Legend and Bishop, Marvin Winans, states, "We're making some bad musical choices, and music gets in your spirit, and we want to have the right thing in our spirit." Bishop Winans made this comment as he was introducing one of his favorite gospel singers, the award-winning Jonathan McReynolds. McReynolds is a young gospel singer with chart topping songs like "Gotta Have You" and "No Gray." His music speaks to challenges people face in their everyday lives and the Christian response towards overcoming these daily struggles. Not only has he garnered the attention of gospel legends like Bishop Winans and Pastor Kim Burrell, but secular artists such as India Arie and the musical genius, Stevie Wonder, are amazed by Jonathan's musical gift and influence.

Interestingly enough, Jonathan's first album was called *Life Music*. All around us, we hear about death in the media, through songs, news broadcast reports, newspapers, and even Facebook. While death is a part of life, let's not forget about life itself. It's time to Speak Life! Adults, youth leaders and parents involved in young people's lives have as much power to speak life as they do to speak death or negativity.

You can create your world with your words. Our world is created by words and is sustained by words. There is an old adage that says, your words become actions, your actions become habits, and your habits become your character. From this statement, I always say, "Say what you want to see, until you see what you said you saw!" As an educator, I see firsthand the effect of words on the children. Students with the best grades, the best behavior and the best attitudes have teachers, parents, and guardians that speak very positively to and about them. Their comments are: "That's my boy!" "My baby girl is smart," "I know my child, and he is not bad," "She loves to read," or "I am proud of him." Most students with the worst grades, worst behavior, and worst attitudes have teachers, parents, and guardians who speak very negatively to and about them. Their normal words about their children are: "She's bad. I don't know what to do with her," "He needs medicine," or "I think he's bipolar." And the list goes on and on, often laced with profanity from some parents. When I hear these comments, I always counteract their words with positive words about their children. Our youth can become what we say, so we have to say the right things no matter what! You cannot survive without words (e.g. reading traffic signs, directions, doctors' reports, medicine bottles, etc.). Since that is the case, we must strive to be intentional about the words we speak. When children misbehave, do not call them bad! The action can be identified as wrong or bad, but don't give them an identity of "bad," based on what they did. Children are not what they do. Train and teach them, and speak life, meaning speak your expectations and your belief, so they can meet them! Speak about what they can be and not so much about what they did! Create a positive future for them with your words and enlist support to help them attain that bright future.

To our youth, do not wait for someone to speak life to you. Create your own positive world with your mouth! If mainstream rappers have enough audacity to speak blasphemous, inappropriate, horrific and terrorizing words, then you should have the courage to speak honorable, encouraging, motivational and life-filled words.

We know that words have power, which is why there is a no snitching movement, because words can affect someone. We also know that words have power because we go to church to hear a preacher give us words. Young people who are brought before a judge because they reenacted the words of mainstream violent songs are sentenced to prison by the word of the judge. It is a sad day when musical instruments that once provided the rhythm for songs are replaced with gunshots, police sirens, and sexual sound effects. Some of the music is force feeding our children murder and pornography in audio form.

The Impact of Speaking Life

The influence and popularity of mainstream hip-hop music increases rapidly! Every month a new song hits the airwaves, becoming the next song heard through the hallways of schools across the country. During my visits, seminars, motivational talks and lectures across the country, I find that once I separate the music (beats, rhythms, and drums, etc.) from the message (lyrics, cues, implications, subliminal information) the artists and the songs are no longer as celebrated.

Many of the seminars I have held with ministers, parents, educators, college students, professors, businessmen and gang members in the crowd have demonstrated the utmost excitement for the recording artists during the beginning of my talks. In every arena I begin with call and response versions of some popular hip-hop songs, censoring the profane language. Overwhelmingly, each audience in every urban and rural community, from some of the lowest poverty communities in the south to middle class regions, knows the lyrics by heart and responds enthusiastically, sharing their affirmation of the music. In most of the churches where I have spoken I've taken a similar approach. I find that the youth choir members always know the uncensored version of the lyrics to the crime-laced songs just as well as they know the worship songs they sing during service. However, once I separate the meaning of the lyrics from the rhythmic flow of the music, I see faces turn from grins and smiles, to expressions of disgust, embarrassment, regret and remorse for what they have been exposing their minds to.

Eric, a young African American male who just began college, had this to say after one of my presentations of the research on mainstream hip-hop music's influence on the youth:

> I just want to thank you, first and foremost, for giving us much more than a cultural event presentation. I was very inspired by the entire presentation. I actually came to the event, because I would receive cultural credit, but I also came because I have to write a paper on a cultural event for a class. What I walked away with was so much more. I have allowed myself to become exposed to a lot of stuff that had no business entering my spirit. When I got back to my residence hall following that presentation, I deleted every song off of my computer with a message that wasn't conducive to feelings of motivation and progression. When I emptied my recycle bin, I cleared 621 songs. I took note that my attitude today was unwaveringly positive. There was even a situation today that arose where I would have normally gotten very upset, but I was pretty mellow. I believe it had a lot to do with

what I allowed to minister to me throughout the day because I am a big fan of music.

Other responses from my various presentations of the research and interactive dialogues resulted in parents apologizing to their children for not effectively screening the music that they purchase or allow them to watch. Many young people have even pledged to no longer listen to music that opposes their positive dreams. The major response from most of the audiences was they were distracted by the beats of the music that they did not think about how derogative the messages are.

Although many responded with the thought that music was having an adverse effect on the youth, some still felt that looking too much into the music is too analytical and that it is possible not to be impacted by the music even though one repeatedly listens to songs with depictions of immoral and illegal acts. The following is the manuscript of Joey, a student at a prestigious university in South Carolina, that references a dialogue between him and another student, centered on my research and presentation to their student body. Joey states:

>...Firstly, I want to thank you for coming and speaking here... I believe you unknowingly fueled the fire inside of our NABSE [National Alliance of Black School Engineers] group by reminding us not only how important others are to us, but how important we are to others. Personally, I drew inspiration from meeting such an articulate and successful young black man...Your presentation on "Weapons of Mass Distraction" was insightful to say the least. I do not listen to any of the artists you displayed in your slideshow, or any similar

artists, because I feel that they promote ideas that go against my religious beliefs. Yet, I believe the presentation allowed people to see past the superficial level of music (meaning just listening to it for the "beat") and to dig more into the content, message, and significance of the music. [I think it was extremely effective that you were young, lively, and relatable. People took your message better because you weren't the guy who hated everything about our generation and looked down on us] ... If you have a song that says "drug dealing music" blasting in your car or you have it as your primary ringtone, you are in fact... advertising that song and consequently the message therein. Whether you accept the message or not is irrelevant in this aspect. If someone wore a shirt that said "Coke," you could very well want a Coke after seeing that shirt, but does that mean that the person wearing the shirt has ever in their life had a Coke? It doesn't. Now, I know no one is perfect, but I believe we should stop making some things "no big deal" and up our standards for ourselves, and one big part of that is to stop sponsoring people who aren't supporting our drive to do better. (Personal communication, April 16, 2010)

I encountered a different experience with a parent that was a part of my presentation. This parent felt that since some of the music is littered with messages that her elementary-aged daughter could not understand, it was acceptable for her child to listen to it, as long as the profane language was censored. My response to that is one day, that child's mind will make inferences and draw conclusions, and while she may not be able to make the respective connections as an elementary school student, it is extremely likely that one day, she will.

Speak Life Strategies

One of the strategies I use to speak life and combat the distracting forces of hip-hop music is to reach the students and surrounding communities in an interactive and engaging way that captures the fascination of the youth through a rap concert. It is important to combat these forces while at the same time, gently protecting the emotions of people who have a great affinity for mainstream hip-hop music. This is called an inspirational/educational rap concert that encourages the parents of young people to listen to music that does not suggest any ideas which would be detrimental if acted upon. This program proved to be a success in the largest elementary school in the school district. It grabbed the attention of and inspired the community. It is called *Empowering the Mind through Rhythm and Rhyme!*

The performers consist of teachers and students in grades Pre-K to fifth. The concept of the show is for students to perform educational and inspirational songs around the following themes: college and career readiness, math, science, reading, social studies, test-taking strategies and having positive self-esteem. Months before the concert, classes were given musical beats, similar to the beats that are used by many of today's popular recording artists. Teachers and students use these beats to write songs about the topics listed above. Students are encouraged to use all their gifts and talents to produce exciting performances. Admission to the concert is free and regular announcements and flyers are sent to parents, students, school board members, the school PTO, community advocates, media outlets, and the greater community.

The response of the school and the community was overwhelmingly positive! The venue was standing room only with a climate of positivity and dynamic rap performances. Several parents and students were interviewed and asked why the event was so important. One father commented that it was good for his daughter to be a part of something positive, though he had been a bit skeptical about having a rap concert at first. Several students shared their joy of rapping positive messages and performing clean dance moves. They relayed how tired they were seeing the provocative girls dancing in music videos and how inappropriate it looks. The theme song of the rap concert contained the following lyrics that I wrote to further define the importance of this concert:

> Young people and parents, I need to let you know
> something, our children are being hoodwinked,
> bamboozled, and tricked, let me explain!
> [Verse 1]
> Give me your ears, I'm putting you on alert
> They say sticks and stones can break bones but
> words don't hurt
> I tell you words do hurt and even more they
> can burn
> When you rapping wicked things that children
> never should learn
> Money they never should earn when they're
> selling that stuff
> I hear it everywhere I go and man enough
> is enough
> 'Cause when the going gets tough the tough

gets going
So I picked up the microphone and out
here flowing
[Chorus]
It's time to empower the mind
No more destroying it with filthiness and songs
about crime
It's time to empower the mind
Wave your hands if you understand the rhythm
and the rhyme
[Verse 2]
I was born with tremendous capabilities
I was born to exceed impossibilities
As great as I am, I still have my humility
'cause I know the One in charge who instilled in me
all my abilities that are designed to change the world
For every man and woman, and every boy and girl
My life is not about me and I hope you see
That every person in this world has a destiny
This is a song that is just to remind
you that you need to empower your mind!

I performed this song with my fourth-grade class as the opening act of the concert. Over five hundred students were involved in this exciting event. Students wore their cool sunglasses as they sang songs with positive lyrics. This event led to some of the students being invited to serve as guest performers on the community awareness show, "Awareness," on the local news station. Viewers from various surrounding areas were impacted by the idea of "empowering the minds" of young people with lyrical content that is designed to help students set and achieve positive goals.

The "Empower the Mind" Music Video

Another strategy for speaking life I use is to help students see that mainstream hip-hop artists aren't the only individuals that can produce and appear in music videos. A group of fifth graders assisted me with the development of a music video for the song, "Empower the Mind!"

The setting was a fifth-grade classroom that was currently in session. The story starts with a young enthusiastic educational advocate who bursts into the classroom in the middle of a lesson and calls for a state of emergency as he emphatically raps about the destructive forces of mainstream hip-hop music. The students and the teacher lean in closely, interested in what he has to say. After the first verse, the students are captivated by their surprise guest and begin singing along with him. The video contains messages centered on setting and attaining goals. It even features a picture of President Barack Obama flashing on the screen. Students and parents now have an inspirational music video to go along with an inspiring song.

Those who have a passion for seeing youth fulfill their God-given destinies have the power to be creative enough to reach our youth. Talk to the youth. Find out what their interests are, and like one of my mentors taught me, "Be crazy about them!" What if we, as youth leaders, went as crazy for them as screaming fans go for their favorite artists? One of the best ways to enhance a negative rap star's performance is to increase his or her fan base. I believe if we increase the support base for our youth, we can also help them enhance their performance. We are in the age now where the child, mother, father, and grandparents can all have the same favorite rappers. Our youth must be taught how to avoid these distractions; as educators and responsible adults we must help to do that work. We cannot afford to be distracted along with them. Do whatever it takes to win our youth! They are worth fighting for and are worth speaking life into.

To Our Youth...
from a Mentor

Chapter Three:
Identity Theft - The Costume Party

Although most of us associate costumes with a holiday on October 31st, many people wear costumes every day of their lives! Weapons of Mass Distraction are influencing the youth to get by in life with disguises, costumes, and alter egos. Weapons of Mass Distraction cause me to believe there is a new answer to the question, "If everyone else jumped off the bridge, would you do it?" There used to be a time when that was a question to ask in order to tell people not to follow the crowd. However, I believe that we are in an age where if that question were posed, with the right beat and in a rhythmic flow, many young people would say, "Yes," as they nod their heads to the music.

Crowds of youth are dressing like their favorite artists, wearing hairstyles like their favorite artists, and even talking like their favorite artists. One particular artist, named Lil' Boosie, wanted his barber to give him a fade and many young people started asking their barbers for the "Boosie Fade." I personally appreciate the haircut, because it is very neat, but consider this: if he has that kind of influence to simply get a haircut and have people follow suit, how much more of an influence would rappers like him have when they produce content that speaks life?

Weapons of Mass Distraction cause young people to be lured away from their purpose. Initially, it was all about getting our youth and their parents to pay money, but when they can get consumers to pay attention in such a way they invest their entire beings into the music, now they have disciples. Our communities are in dangerous places when Weapons of Mass Distraction create disciples out of music fans.

The Day I Almost Joined the Costume Party

Sometimes I feel like I am in a twilight zone movie because many older elementary school students, middle school students, college students and even some young parents are all dressing alike. Our youth often find more security in the music they listen to than they do in the adults who take care of them. At least they can count on the music always being there, saying the same thing, and sounding cool while doing it. It is very hard to tell who is influencing whom because so many young people are talking alike, walking alike, and dressing alike. There is often pressure for youth leaders to appear to be like the youth to reach them, but I disagree with that notion. We do not have to become the world to win the world. Compassion, consistency, relevance, and love will win them over.

As a child, I was constantly bullied by fellow classmates and older guys who were considered cool. These were the guys that had all the girls, the name brand clothes, and the attitudes that made people fear them. Many of the guys wore loose-fitting clothes and their caps backwards. I was the kid that was dressed by his mother, ironed pants, crisp buttoned-down shirts and a clean haircut given by his mother. The teachers loved me, but many of the cool kids saw me as a target and the brunt of their jokes. Sometimes, when I was alone in my room I would put on a baseball cap, sag my pants and practice walking and dressing like the "cool kids." In the mirror, I would transform into a kid that the "cool kids" would love, at the expense of becoming someone I was not. It was very simple and did not require much effort. In fact, it was harder to be myself than to be someone else. During my "costume rehearsals" I realized although being someone else was easy, I did not feel free because my style, attitude, and character were being dictated by someone else. So I turned my hat back around, pulled up my pants, tucked my shirt in and continued being me.

About fifteen years later, I would conduct the experiment again. No, I wasn't having flashbacks of being bullied, but as a youth speaker I was asked to speak at a worship service, and to make a point, I decided to join the costume party that had grown much larger since I left middle school. Instead of coming to the church dressed in a suit, I came dressed as a thugged out hustler looking for a record deal. I wore a bandana that covered the bottom of my face, and a du-rag with a fitted cap on my head turned backwards. I wore a shirt that was 3 times my size that had the image of a man's face with a set of gold teeth in his mouth. On top of that I wore a biker's jacket. On the bottom, I wore jeans three times my size, sagging far below my bottom (my shirt was so long that even though the top of my pants was to my knees, you could not see my underwear—even though sagging and showing underwear has become massively influential—I will not go that far to make a point), and untied timberland boots. The last item I put on, to seal my perfect hip-hop attire were shades. I embraced a negative and thuggish attitude. It wasn't hard because the attire almost carried with it a spirit of rebellion. When I arrived at the church, I was greeted nicely by some ushers, but I ignored "those haters" and went to a seat in the back of the church. I arrived during praise and worship, so I kicked back and waited for them to bring up the speaker.

I received many stares, but no one came to talk to me, told me to remove my hat or anything. A lot of the young people were looking at me, adults were looking at me through their peripheral vision, and some men in the front of the church seemed to keep their eyes on me. Now it was time for the speaker. When the youth leader of the church stood up and began introducing the "speaker," I immediately stood up and began to cut him off, shouting random rude things. I was loud and obnoxious! The youth leader was shocked and couldn't continue. I took the microphone, and began to speak about costumes, as I was disrobing. When I took off my costume, I had my suit underneath. Everyone was astonished. I began talking to them about the power of images and how our youth are attracted to threatening and obnoxious images and how we as youth leaders subconsciously co-sign these depictions. Later in the book, I will share the rest of the story and the response of the church. However, it was amazing for them to see that what was on the outside was in no way related to what was on the inside.

If we live by what we see long enough, we will develop a surface mentality that is only satisfied by what we see and feel. I relayed to the congregation that people with identity crises need ministry too. Don't let their hard or inappropriate exteriors distract you from the opportunity to offer help to hurting souls. Weapons of Mass Distraction influence more than our young people. They can also prevent leaders from being sensitive to the needs of our youth and some rappers because of their costumes.

Chapter Four:
Unholy MatriMONEY

"It feels like my lady is the money/ I wish I could have a baby with the money/ I can't leave the house without her on me/ You know that I'm married to the money, the money" This is the chorus from a song by Award-winning, hip-hop recording artist Trey Songz. The song, "Married to the Money" refers to money as a spouse that Songz fell in love with and can't live without. Songz is not the only musical artist who describes this experience. In an interview on ESPN's *Highly Questionable*, a sports talk television program, Rap mogul, Birdman, answers a question about the rumor that he sleeps on a million dollars. Birdman answers, "I still sleep on a million dollars cash. That's just a 'fatuation for me in life. I do that and I'mma do that until I die."

As a mentor, it is difficult to see young people chasing money before they even know who they are. As an educator who has worked in some of South Carolina's poorest neighborhoods, I often find myself apologizing to students on behalf of mainstream's famous rappers because I watch these young people with broken chains linked together with safety pins, aluminum foil in their mouths to resemble gold teeth, try to look as flashy or as rich as the mainstream rappers they admire. This behavior comes from a poverty mentality. Students from impoverished neighborhoods see money as their way out. There is some truth to that. But because poverty can come with an accompanying mentality, many people with this mindset have the power to make the money, but lack the character to manage it wisely, and they increase the quantity (of money or possessions) in their lives without improving the quality of their lives.

A famous rapper that has much of my students' attention is YoungBoy, formerly, NBA YoungBoy. The NBA in the former name stands for Never Broke Again. In an interview with, *The FADER*, a popular hip-hop magazine, YoungBoy says, "I hated school. My mind wasn't right there. I really don't think it's important. I got money without school." One of his final statements in the interview is, "I really don't give a f--k about school." With millions of followers on social media, the message has a multiplier effect on a generation of young people that are in school physically, but could possibly be checked out mentally. I don't want to choose their role models for them, but I want them to be strong enough to make decisions that lead to life. When today's hit rap songs are themed with guns, drugs, murder, prostitution and uncontrollable behavior, all to make money, I am not "okay" with calling it *just* music.

Students I work with right now are echoing YoungBoy's words in the classroom, and these students are only 8- and 9-year-olds. Words have power, which is why YoungBoy has millions of views and followers on social media. His words have become points of meditation for our youth who can relate to his youthfulness. In my office, I speak with families who are just as concerned as I am about the words coming out of their children's mouths when the music is not playing.

Our youth must understand that money doesn't define a human being and that they are more valuable than riches. To commit lewd acts for money, steal for money, kill for money, and risk death for money implies that the value of money is greater than the value of human life.

While this music has provided many people with a ticket out of crime and poverty, it has also helped to lead many people into a life of crime and poverty.

The Value of YOU: You Are One of a Kind

In 2003, I had the privilege of serving as the National Pre-Alumni Council (NPAC) President of the United Negro College Fund and was a featured panelist at the Rainbow Push Coalition's Citizen's Education Fund Conference. This experience afforded me the opportunity to meet individuals such as Michael Jordan's mother, Deloris Jordan, Judge Greg Mathis, and many others. During a luncheon at the conference, I sat next to an Illinois State Senator, and we engaged in a stimulating conversation about education. He seemed intrigued by my passion to be an educator. I was equally impressed with him and his leadership. During the luncheon, many celebrities were recognized, and as great as my table partner seemed to be, the Reverend Jesse Jackson and actor Danny Glover, who were on stage, never announced him as a special guest. After the luncheon, we parted ways, but before leaving he shook my hand, looked me in the eye and said, "Hayward, you are a fine young man." I thanked him and asked him if I could have a picture with him. I wanted a picture to remember him, because we shared such a great conversation. A few years later, an African American man appeared on several news outlets announcing his bid for presidential candidate for the 2008 election. As I watched the announcement, and heard his voice, I was immediately reminded of the young senator I met in 2003 in Chicago. When he gave me his card, I remember his name was very unusual and hard to pronounce. I looked at my photo album and matched the picture with the gentleman in the media who happened to be Senator Barack Obama. When I met him in the summer of 2003 he was not widely known, but that didn't matter because he knew who he was. It is amazing to think that for about an hour, I was sitting next to someone who would one day shake up the world as the first Black president of the United States of America. Although no one at the luncheon knew this, it didn't mean he was not a valuable person with something to contribute. You never know who you might be sitting next to!

When I tell my story to audiences of how I met President Obama before the world knew him as president, I also tell them how one of my best friends says, "President Obama met YOU!" He says this to remind me of how great I am. Do not be distracted by people's celebrity status to the point you lose sight of the fact that they could be meeting you. My pastor, Apostle Shane Wall, says, "People are only famous because a lot of people know who they are." Just because you are not famous, doesn't mean you are of lesser value. It would not have been possible for President Obama to achieve what has never been achieved if he was given to distraction. This doesn't mean he didn't make mistakes or was never distracted, but what it demonstrates is that he always came back to focus on his purpose!

So I urge our young people, turn off the radio, take the headphones out of your ears and spend time answering the following questions: What am I good at? What am I passionate about? What is my purpose? Identifying one's purpose is easy. I believe, as individuals we have a common purpose, which is to help others. However, the method and niche by which we achieve our common purpose and the people we are called to help are determined by our talents, gifts, abilities, and our time on this earth.

Achieving our potential successfully is getting the proper instructions to accomplish our purpose from God. We are made with everything we need to accomplish our purpose and to do it God's way. In addition, as much as we like to sustain our lives with food, true life is found in our ability to yield to the instructions of our creator. Deuteronomy 8:3 of the Bible says that, "man does not live by bread alone," but man lives by every word that proceeds from the mouth of the Lord. The more we are in contact with the One that created us, the more in touch we will be with our purpose and our reason for existence. While helping people is the broader sense of our purpose, God will make clear to us specifically what that means in each of our lives.

The path to discovering how one will fulfill his/her purpose takes longer than others. My advice is to keep serving and helping others. While you are doing that, you will collide with your life's calling. I have helped countless people with this same principle and it has strengthened their focus and caused them to live life with intentionality. As a result, they experience satisfaction and excitement every day because they have a reason to live. Know that no matter what people say about you, good or bad, you are not an accident. You were created for something unique and special. Like President Obama, you have within you the ability to do what has never been done!

What's Your A.I.M.?

Any person yearning for fulfillment in life needs A.I.M. to live a life of purpose that will combat Weapons of Mass Distraction. As a young person who wants purpose in life, you will do well to develop *Aspirations*, look for *Inspiration*, and discover your *Motivation*. A.I.M. will help you rule out the distractions, so you can maximize your potential. If you do not possess A.I.M. in this war zone of a society, you will find yourself M.I.A. on the battlefield of life!

Aspiration is the hope or ambition of achieving something. Be a visionary. Dream! Declutter your mind and spirit from the debris of the Weapons of Mass Distraction. Dream and desire something beyond what can be seen with the naked eye. This will help you to assess what you are good at and what you are capable of. Aspiring to be rich limits your view. Life is worth more than a paycheck. When you realize who you are, you will see you have legendary status when it comes to purpose. When one thinks of President Obama, one does not think of wealth but of legacy. There is no price tag on your legacy. The root of aspiration is "aspire," which means to seek to attain or accomplish a particular goal. Your goal is not coming to you, you must go to it.

What is one thing basketball, football, and soccer all have in common? They all have a goal. Every time a team steps on the court or the field to play, there are opponents trying to stop them from reaching their goals. Soccer even has a goalie whose only job is to stand in front of the goal to protect it from the offensive team. When you go after your goals, this action is offensive to Weapons of Mass Distraction. Whether it is the negative music whispering sweet nothings in your ear, or bullies and other negative people in your way, remember, these are your opponents. You can defeat your opponents with a good coach and team members with the same passion. We all need a mentor to let us know what is possible and to help us navigate through challenges and opposing forces that will try to stop us from achieving our goals. The late Dr. Benjamin E. Mays was a civil rights activist and former president of Morehouse College during the time Dr. Martin L. King, Jr. attended the college. He was a tremendous leader in our country and was also known for serving as a mentor to Dr. King. If Dr. King needed a mentor, certainly all of us desiring to reach goals need mentors as well. Align yourself with a group that challenges you to grow in order to accomplish your goals. When you are part of a team, you realize you are not alone. In addition to all this, you must not doubt! You must speak life to your vision daily! You must say what you want to see, until you see what you said you saw!

Aspiration

1. Be a Visionary: Dream, Hope, Desire and set goals.

2. Find a Mentor, and join a team that will help you achieve your goals.

3. Speak Life to your vision! Say what you want to see, until you see it.

While Aspiration is more external, Inspiration is internal. Inspiration is the action or power of moving the intellect or emotions. Weapons of Mass Distraction constantly try to do this by suggesting content that potentially inspires our youth to aspire to false definitions of success. However, our youth need responsible peers and adults in their lives that will inspire them to be someone that can make positive contributions to our society. The greatest resources for youth are positive and inspiring role models.

Earlier I mentioned even Dr. King had a mentor, but his mentor was qualified to be his mentor because he provided inspiration for him that would guide him towards his destiny. Dr. King was so inspired and convinced of his purpose that no opponent, not even the fear of death, could distract him from reaching his goal. The root of inspiration is inspire—to influence, to move, or guide by divine or supernatural means. One of Dr. King's greatest quotes references Matthew 23:11, "He who is greatest among you shall be your servant" (AMPC). Inspirational people serve! It is important to be inspired by true greatness, which is true service to others. In the medical sense of the word, inspiration also means to inhale. Our parents, teachers and youth leaders must be watchful of what our youth inhale into their minds and spirits. Our youth must inhale an atmosphere of positivity.

Inspiration

1. Listen to positive words of life!
2. Protect your identity! (Don't allow pop culture and negativity to define you.)
3. Serve others!

Leaders, Aspiration and Inspiration are no good if our youth and adults who love them do not have Motivation. Motivation is the act or process of giving someone a reason for doing something. The root, motive, is something (as a need or desire) that causes a person to act. Because our young people are more valuable than money, and it is impossible to put a price tag on their or anyone's greatness, money should not be their motivation. Their talents, gifts, and abilities are given to them in order to engage, educate, and empower people to make life better for others. There is no amount of money that can truly pay them for the ability to serve. We must help them understand they are more valuable than money. To me, going to work with money as a motivation is sophisticated prostitution, where one uses all his/her talents, gifts, and abilities for a paycheck. I want our youth to be so empowered that if they were offered a 3.5-million-dollar salary to do what they do best, they are able to tell the employer, "Sir, I am worth much more than that...but I'll take it!" They should not be silly and leave the money, but they should take it with the mentality that the employer is not buying them, and they are not in an unholy matriMONEY relationship! Motivation should be greater than money, but could include money. Young people, there is nothing wrong with making a lot of money, but you must not place that above fulfilling your purpose. When you have an inappropriate relationship with finances you lose sight of your God-given assignment to serve people. Make sure money has its proper place in your life and that it is not the motivation, otherwise it will easily desensitize you to the needs of others. When you are motivated by helping others while using your gifts to do it, you won't have to chase money because the money will chase you!

Motivation

1. Follow your purpose and the money will follow you! Money is not the endgame.
2. Be intentional about your purpose! Know what it is and why it is yours to fulfill.
3. Set goals and celebrate your achievement of them!

The Power to A.I.M. will prevent Weapons of Mass Distraction from taking your eyes off the prize—discovering and fulfilling your purpose. You might say, "Well, I know someone who is very successful, very positive, and they listen to all types of music including negative hip-hop music." My response is, as great as this person is, how much greater could s/he be without the negativity they have consumed? If someone can truly accomplish unprecedented things while being given to Weapons of Mass Distraction, how much more would s/he be able to accomplish without them?

To the Congregation… from a Minister

Chapter Five:
Lyrical Electrocution: A Weapon of Mass Distraction

They are everywhere, and they have become one of the most popular accessories donned by the youth! Professional athletes are wearing them! You can see young people wearing them while driving, shopping, and walking with their parents in grocery stores. Very rarely will you see young mainstream hip-hop listeners without their headphones!

When I am called to speak at youth rallies, conferences, and worship services, I will sometimes do skits to introduce points I intend to make. One of the skits I perform uses headphones. Once I am introduced, I put on my headphones, grab a chair, and place it in front of the church as I am talking. I then sit down in the chair, hook the headphones to my smartphone as if I am about to listen to music, and then I start rapping and shaking uncontrollably as if I am being electrocuted in front of the audience, resembling being in an electric chair. The point I make is that many of our young people are listening to content that is frying their brains, much like electricity affects the natural body when it is in contact with an electric current for an extended period. We are witnessing the Lyrical Electrocution of our youth. We are watching them die, right before our eyes as electric currents carry life threatening, lyrical content through circuits in the headphone cables directly into their minds.

Electrocution, according to Webster, is to kill a person by electric shock. *The Burn Survivor Resource Center* states,

> Electrocution injuries can result in a variety of wounds, and sometimes in death. Factors that determine the extent and severity of electrocution injuries include the type of current, the duration of

contact with the current, the pathway of electricity through the body, the type of circuit and amount of voltage encountered.

The following physical body systems are adversely impacted by electrocution: Cardiovascular system, Respiratory System, Central Nervous System, the Musculoskeletal System, and the Integumentary System. The aforementioned systems mirror the consciousness that is also negatively affected and could hinder someone from reaching their fullest potential for the sake of some bomb beats and deadly lyrical distractions. Let's take a look at how each of these systems can be negatively affected by mainstream hip-hop music.

The cardiovascular system contains essential components such as the heart, blood, and blood vessels. A natural electrical current can cause it to shut down. Lyrical Electrocution is causing the hearts of our young people to be cold and they are almost made to believe that life itself has no value. Hip-hop artist, 21 Savage has a song called, "No Heart" and is even quoted in the song stating, "I grew up in these streets without no heart… wet your mama's house, wet your grandma's house, keep shootin' until somebody die." In other words, many rappers' music has no heart and no regard for the quality of human life. We must show them it is cool to love your neighbor. We need each other! Our youth will not learn the value of life until we teach them.

Responsible for breathing, the respiratory system can hardly stand the shock of an electrocution. However, in Lyrical Electrocution, the breath of life in our youth is compromised with the inhalation of death lyrics which adversely affects the spiritual (breath of) life in our youth. Genesis 2:7 of the Bible states, "And the Lord God formed man of the dust of the ground and breathed into his nostrils the breath of life; and man became a living soul." It takes breath to speak, and we have all been given God's breath. So, if God created us with His breath, the breath used to speak should sound like Him. I am sure God did not breathe the breath of murder, sexual immorality, stealing and profanity in us. It doesn't make sense to use what God gave us to offend Him and the others He made. Lyrical Electrocution drives out the breath of God, which is the real life of man.

The musculoskeletal system is made up of muscles, cartilage, tendons, ligaments, and joints and other connective tissue. In other words, when this system is destroyed, the body falls apart. Many of the songs of the mainstream hip-hop artists come from moments when they felt like all was lost. Earlier in this book, we read Biggie Smalls' rap about wanting to die. As rich and famous as he was, he showed signs of a lot of internal, spiritual pain. This type of pain can be transferred to impressionable youth. Music about death, revenge, suicide, and drug addiction is a Weapon of Mass Distraction with the ability to drive people away from the proper ways of seeking support (i.e. talking with a pastor, mentor, teacher and yielding to their support until they can "pull it all together") and encourages them to illegally self-medicate, give in to peer pressure and to live fast and die young.

The integumentary system is the organ system made up of the skin and soft tissues. Electrocution can affect the sensory receptors to detect pain, sensation, pressure, and temperature. The more listeners are exposed to the horrific, terrorizing and sexually explicit content in mainstream hip-hop music, the more they become desensitized to the world around them making it more and more difficult to empathize with the pain of their neighbors even to the point of laughing at people's pain. Many murderous lines contain mockeries of mothers crying at their sons' funerals who were victims of homicides. When the youth are inundated with lyrics about this behavior, they become numb and unaware of the impact that some of these words can have. It takes less than a second to fire off a deadly lyric, and it takes the same amount of time to discharge a deadly firearm.

The central nervous system, which contains the brain and spinal cord, is the motherboard of the body. The spinal cord, in regard to Lyrical Electrocution, could be considered the ability the youth and those who love them must have to stand up against the lies and the poison being presented to them every minute. Weapons of Mass Distraction weakens the backbones of our young people causing them to fear no one but the police. It is funny how the songs often talk about running from no one, but the police. They fight each other, curse their mothers, disown their fathers, and abuse women, but when cops come around they scatter like roaches when the light switch is turned on. This is no disrespect to policemen, but it references the childlike mentality of these artists. They have the least respect for those they should have the most respect for. Their backbones have been shattered by the shrapnel of bomb beats and weakened by Lyrical Electrocution.

Lyrical Electrocution also distracts the mind in such a way that it influences the mind to imagine the individual is someone they are not. This is evident by the number of people living double lives and thinking nothing of it because, "music makes me lose control," as stated in Hip-hop star Missy Elliot's song, "Lose Control." While this is not the only reason people live double lives, it does lead one to ask the question: how could my mind process songs about killing, but I cry when I go to someone's funeral who was murdered. A few years ago, I attended the funeral of a fourteen-year-old gunned down, but many of the young people who mourned the death of the young male are fans of some of the music that affirms very similar killings. The United Negro College Fund's motto is, "A Mind is a Terrible Thing to Waste." We must do a better job at helping the youth to value their minds, because if they do not use them wisely, they will lose them miserably. Brain research suggests that when the brain is not exposed to meaningful content, it will waste away, otherwise known as brain atrophy. When the brain feels it is not needed, it starts to shrink in size. How much of our young people's minds are being "wasted" because of Weapons of Mass Distraction?

Carter G. Woodson, historian, author, and journalist writes in his book, *The Mis-Education of the Negro*,

> When you control a man's thinking you do not have to worry about his actions. You do not have to tell him not to stand here or go yonder. He will find his 'proper place' and will stay in it. You do not need to send him to the back door. He will go without being told. In fact, if there is no back door, he will cut one for his special benefit. His education makes it necessary.

It is evident that our youth are being mis-educated, misinformed, and taken advantage of by Weapons of Mass Distraction through mainstream hip-hop. Our youth are making it necessary to listen to this type of music, evidenced by the number of hours a day the youth spend on YouTube listening to and watching the videos. There are many adults who criticize me for my passion for helping our youth make positive choices about what they listen to. They say, "They are just kids, and it is all in fun." While they are "having fun," negative hip hop music is robbing them of their identities in "record" time. If it is the beat the youth want to hear, the following artists have amazing beats and the flows to match that will positively empower the youth, while giving them something to dance to. These artists are: Lecrae, Trip Lee, Da Truth, Ambassador, The Cross Movement, Andy Mineo, Datin, Bizzle, and a host of other rappers. These artists happen to be some of my favorite rap artists and their lyrics are clean, relevant, and powerful! My oldest son loves them too.

We rescue our youth from the Lyrical Electrocution by helping them understand that although it is difficult to avoid some of the content, they can control their ability to put on the headphones. It is time for us, as responsible adults, to wake up and be more sensitive to what we allow into our youth's hearts and minds.

To Parents...
from a Father

Chapter Six:
Smoke Signals: Do You Hear Me? Do You See Me?

When I hear a lot of this music and think of many of the artists, I'm reminded of the movie Castaway. The lead character had a good family and job and, suddenly, his life changed due to a traumatic experience—plane crash). This plane crash left everyone dead except the lead character. To try to get help, he created smoke signals, to get potential flying planes' attention. That is how I feel about a lot of rappers. Many of them were hurt as children. They seem like castaways, trying to get the attention from those that are free. It is not their fault they grew up the way they did. It is not their fault they were hurt through fatherlessness, molestation, divorce, peer pressure, etc. However, it is against street code to show weakness and cry on Dr. Phil's couch, and it's cooler to make fun of Uncle Phil in order to mask your pain. It is also much cooler to not let them see you cry real tears, so they cry tattooed tears. They cry bullets. They cry misogynistic lyrics. Some female rappers have different cries. They cry about how much dudes want to have sex with them, about how big their booties are, and how good sex is to them. Does anyone hear them? Turn off the beats for a minute. Listen to them. Wouldn't it be silly, if a man flying in an airplane saw the lone survivor on a desert island throwing up flares, and he gave the man a thumbs-up, "good job," took a picture of it, and posted it on Instagram, bragging about how he saw this cool guy shooting fireworks on an island as he was flying by? The flares were not for a "show." He was trying to get the pilot's attention, but the pilot did not see that; all he saw was entertainment. As adults we must be sensitive to the smoke signals. Money, cars, clothes, and houses do not make rappers eternally happy. We cannot be distracted by their confidence in rap videos and the power in their voice over the radios. Many rappers say, "My pain got me the success." Well, pain can't take people to a healthy place, it is a signal that something is wrong. For many rappers, pain is their content and it causes them to be unhealthy in their souls, though many of them are enjoying the material possessions that come with it. They do not last forever. I hear them and I am praying for them. While praying for them, I am still making it clear to youth that following them will lead them to an unhealthy place in their souls.

More than Music

Former contributor for the Pittsburgh Post-Gazette, Kathy SaeNgian, writes about the research of Dr. Carolyn West in her article that expresses the exploitation of young adolescents in hip-hop music. Dr. Carolyn M. West is the Professor of Psychology and Division Chair of the Social, Behavioral and Human Sciences in the School of Interdisciplinary Arts and Sciences at the University of Washington Tacoma.

In this article, Dr. West states "What's changed over time is the greater sexualization of hip-hop. Initially, it started off as a revolutionary form of music. Now, large corporations produce images that sell, and there is a blatant link between hip-hop and pornography."

Since mainstream hip-hop is a male-dominated genre, I am uniquely concerned about young and adolescent females. They are bombarded with images in media that suggest and force inaccurate and degrading images for young ladies to accept.

Many artists argue that the problem does not lie with them, but with their parents. However, the reality of it is most of their fans and revenue are generated by individuals who are too underdeveloped to make responsible decisions about what they are listening to. I work in the communities where many of the youth and their families live and die by the negative content portrayed in the music, and it is difficult for many parents to censor the content for their children, partly because they too are drawn to the negative content themselves.

I speak to countless audiences of people who agree with everything I say about the negativity in hip-hop music and can even add to my commentary and speeches. However, there is a gap between what people understand and what people stand for when it comes to suggestive content that causes young people to transform right before our very eyes. It has become more than music, it has become a way of life.

The Father Factor in Weapons of Mass Distractions

Many rappers' defense to allegations of negatively inspiring the youth is that parents are primarily responsible for raising their children, not the hip-hop industry. Rappers such as LL Cool J know what it's like to grow up without both biological parents, particularly without his father. I know firsthand the pain caused by growing up without my father and being raised by my single-parent mother. In my interview with Gordon Roberts on the 700 Club, I describe how forgiving my father for not being in my life freed me from a life of anger and resentment. Like LL Cool J and me, so many former and present-day rappers can relate to growing up without their fathers including Lil' Wayne, TuPac, Notorious B.I.G., Meek Mill, Beanie Sigel, and Jay-Z among others. If you listen closely enough, you can hear some of the content coming from rappers about the pain of growing up with an absent father.

Award-winning rapper Meek Mill raps about the pain

of losing his father as a toddler in the song, "Traumatized." He raps, "When I find the n---a that killed my daddy know Ima ride/ Hope you hear me/ Ima kill you n---a to let you know that I don't feel you n---a/ Yeah, you ripped my family apart and made my momma cry/ so when I see you n---a it's gon' be a homicide/ Cuz I was only a toddler, you left me traumatized…"

Grammy Award-Winning Rap Mogul Shawn Corey Carter, a.k.a. Jay-Z, and rapper Beanie Siegel, also penned and recorded a song about their pain of having an absent father in the song, "Where Have You Been?" In the song, Jay-Z sings, "I would say 'my daddy loves me and he'll never go away"/ Bulls—t, do you even remember December's my birthday?/ Do you even remember the tender boy/You turned into a cold young man/ With one goal and one plan/ Get mommy out of some jam, she was always in one…". He goes on to say, "You said that you was comin' through/ I would stay in the hallway (waitin')/ Always playing the bench (waitin')/ And that day came and went/ F—K YOU! Very much you showed me the worst kind of pain." I am convinced through over 10 years of studying mainstream hip-hop, many rappers today are traumatized.

In an interview with Oprah Winfrey, Jay-Z sat down and shared some very specific details about the pain of disconnecting with his father at the age of 11. In the interview Oprah asked, "When you were 5, your family moved to the Marcy projects— and then your father left when you were 11. When you look back at that, what did your 11-year-old self feel?" Jay-Z's response was, "Anger. At the whole situation. Because when you're growing up, your dad is your superhero. Once you've let yourself fall that in love with someone, once you put him on such a high pedestal and he lets you down, you never want to experience that pain again. So, I remember just being really quiet and really cold. Never wanting to let myself get close to someone like that again. I carried that feeling throughout my life, until my father and I met up before he died."

Regarding Jay-Z's anger, Oprah asked if he knew he was angry. Jay-Z responded with, "Yeah. I also felt protective of my mom. I remember telling her, 'Don't worry, when I get big, I'm going to take care of this.' I felt like I had to step up. I was 11 years old, right? But I felt I had to make the situation better."

"How did that change you?" Oprah asked, and Jay-Z answered "It made me not express my feelings as much. I was already a shy kid, and it made me a little reclusive. But it also made me independent. And stronger. It was a weird juxtaposition."

At the age of 12, Jay-Z shot his brother in the shoulder. Oprah asked, "Did your father's leaving have anything to do with that? Did it turn you into the kind of angry kid who would end up shooting his brother?" Jay-Z's response was "Yes—and my brother was dealing with a lot of demons... He was doing a lot of drugs. He was taking stuff from our family. I was the youngest, but I felt like I needed to protect everybody."

Sometimes the youth and fans of all ages forget that the rappers they idolize are human beings with issues. While growing up without his father, and admittedly sharing that he was angry and cold, he sold drugs during his teenage and young adult years. In addition to hustling, he was also rapping. Out of his pain, he sold drugs, and out of his pain, he rapped to the masses.

Oprah states to Jay-Z in the interview, "In one of your songs, you wrote that you weren't sure if your father even remembered your birthday is in December." "I believed that." Jay-Z answered, "When I was a kid, I once waited for him on a bench. He never showed up. Even as an adult, that affected me. So, when my mom set up this meeting, I told her he wouldn't come—and the first time, he didn't. At that point, I was really done, but Mom pushed for another meeting, because she's just a beautiful soul." Oprah responds with, "The second time, your father showed up." Jay-Z answers, "He showed up. And I gave him the real conversation. I told him how I felt the day he left. He was saying stuff like 'Man, you knew where I was.' I'm like, 'I was a kid! Do you realize how wrong you were? It was your responsibility to see me.' He finally accepted that."

Putting the "Hood" Back in Fatherhood

A "hood" is a protective covering. Cars have hoods to protect the engines. Many coats and sweatshirts have hoods to protect heads and necks to prevent people from catching colds. To me, "father-hood," denotes that fathers are to protect their children from any sort of harm, including these Weapons of Mass Distractions that are trying to take them out. They were indeed created to be heroes. It is like the word is a command: Father, cover! While Jay-Z and his father were able to patch things up in his adult years, only a couple of months before his father died, look at all the time spent without his "hero."

When Oprah asked Jay-Z about selling drugs as a youth, Jay-Z's response was, "As a kid, I didn't know any better. But now, if I were to act as if what I did wasn't bad, that would be irresponsible. And I'd have to bear the weight of that." How many young rappers today are rapping about criminal lives not knowing any better because they lack the parenting necessary to teach them the way? Better yet, how many of our youth are being distracted by the detrimental content of many of today's rap songs because they do not have their "father-hood" to protect them from these "entertaining" attacks? Our society of young people is almost becoming a blind-leading-the-blind world. We are leaving our youth to fend for themselves, and they do not have the tools to handle life without a savior—a hero.

Regarding the time Jay-Z sold drugs, Oprah references Maya Angelou and shares that she always says, "When you know better, you do better. Do you still think back on that time in your life?" "All the time." Jay-Z responds, "When you make music, you're constantly on the psychiatrist's couch, so to speak. That's an outlet for me. Because I'm not normally a talkative person. I don't have conversations like this for no reason."

Many people may not believe me when I say it is not just music, but my interpretation of the comments of those who some call the "greatest rapper alive" implies that his music is indeed more than entertainment. In the literal construction of the word, "hood" is a suffix that denotes a quality or condition. So, what is the condition or quality of fatherhood in our society? According to the U.S. Census Bureau's 2016 Current Population Survey Annual Social and Economic Supplement, 17.2 million children live in father-absent homes with their mother only. According to the National Center for Fathering, 71% of high school dropouts come from fatherless homes, while 71% of teenage pregnancies also come from fatherless homes. There is nothing like the bond between a father and his daughter. As the father of a daughter, my protective radar increased when she was born. Not only do I protect her physically, but I am also her emotional protector, guarding her from lies and deceit that would try to distract her from her natural beauty within. Without this type of "hood," our youth have slim chances for success. According to the National Center for Father's Fathering in America Poll, in 72.2 % of the

U.S. population, fatherlessness is the most significant family or social problem.

Aside from the millions of fathers absent from homes, millions more are present, but are emotionally absent or providing a bad influence for their children. Fatherlessness is an epidemic and it takes more than biological fathers to now protect our youth. We need positive men to step up and defend them!

The Irresponsibility of Hip-Hop Music

In a January 2005 *Essence* article entitled, "Take Back the Music," Dr. Carolyn West is quoted saying, "We live in America, so people have a right to produce those images, so I am not talking about censorship. But even if the artists won't be responsible, the community has to hold them accountable." The images Dr. West speaks of are pornographic, violent and other criminal images that seem to be almost mandatory components of hit records in hip-hop.

I remember serving as the keynote speaker at a youth empowerment summit for one thousand plus middle schoolers. To engage the audience prior to my speech, the event featured chants, a mascot dancing and music. The young people were having so much fun chanting, dancing, and rapping to the music. As I listened closely, I realized the students were singing along to songs about gang activity, sex and drugs. The artists being played before I addressed the audience were Cardi B, 21 Savage and O.T. Genesis.

How is it that students can sing about gang violence at a youth empowerment summit? The answer is the beats are so catchy and popular that people feel pressured to have a good time by playing what the children want to hear, even if it is not good for them. So many people believe the only thing that matters is the beat. The reality of it is, long after the beat stops, the song continues to play in the minds of our youth. I want the artists to know their lavish lifestyles are built on the backs of their fans, young people who are following the example of what their lyrics describe. With such a massive following of young people buying their music, listening to their songs, and watching their videos, artists have ample opportunity to use their influence to responsibly and consistently share with the youth how to positively overcome adversity.

Too often, rappers defend their negative lyrics with the statement, "I'm like a reporter. I'm just reporting what goes on in the hood." While that may be true, many of our youth already know what's going on in the hood and do not need it reinforced with a beat behind it. Some of the young people I work with daily live out the lyrics they rap, and at the funerals I've attended, I've found these victims' families don't appreciate the community's insensitivity to negative and violent lyrics. Music that continues to promote violence desensitizes our youth to violence. Until the crimes happen against these young people or their close relatives, the violence seems as insignificant to them as the injury or death of a player in a video game.

I am convinced that many rappers are traumatized by having witnessed heinous crimes, losing family members to drugs and gun violence, and living without their fathers during their youth. Since a lot of them use music as therapy (and happen to become famous as a result), they think they are now "okay" because they have "made it." However, fame for many of them does nothing for the trauma. Rather, it distracts them and even numbs them from the pain experienced from such a traumatic life. From their content, though they are often smiling in their videos, it is very clear that many rappers are still hurting. Instead of admitting their hurt and working to transform their experiences into something positive and life-affirming, many artists reflect the violence and pain that have traumatized them back into their art for the world to witness, never considering how this content will affect their fans, many of whom are youth still impressionable and vulnerable.

Chapter Seven:
Overprotection Is Not a Sin

One of the most inspirational books for graduates happens to be a children's book called, *Oh the Places You'll Go*. The book talks about the journey of life and its challenges, and the potential to go to great places because of one's abilities. It also talks about the power one possesses to make wise choices. Weapons of Mass Distraction in hip hop music are taking our youth places they are not permitted to go.

The pornographic content of hip-hop songs is accessible to children under 21, and these same children are not allowed into establishments that promote this degrading activity, such as strip clubs. Instead of the recording artists taking our youth to the clubs, the artists (through their artistry) are taking the clubs to our youth. In school, we tell children, "Read books, because they take you places you may have never been and expose you to new things that you have never seen before." That concept can also apply to music videos because these images feed a child's very sensitive imagination. If they can believe in Santa Claus, the Easter Bunny, and the Tooth Fairy, it certainly isn't hard for them to see real people in music videos and believe in everything they say.

Award-winning rapper and actor, Shad Moss, also known as Bow Wow, grew up in hip-hop. He credits his mother for his introduction to hip-hop. When he was 5 years old, his mother took him to a concert in Columbus, Ohio to hear Snoop Dogg and Dr. Dre on the "Chronic Tour." "Chronic," in this sense, is weed laced with cocaine. His mother was young, according to Moss, and the concert host was entertaining the crowd and asked who wanted to come to the stage to rap. His mother held Moss up to get the host to pick him. Moss was chosen and Snoop Dogg and Dr. Dre found out about the "kid on stage during intermission." They invited him back and asked him to go on tour with these artists without the supervision of the mother. Some years later, a star was born and his name was Lil' Bow Wow. Bow Wow says his major rap influences were west coast gangster rappers. He was even nicknamed Kid Gangster as a child.

Shad Moss' story of becoming Kid Gangster to ultimately Lil' Bow Wow is evidence of hip-hop music's powerful influence on young people. Having a young child tour with Snoop Dogg and Dr. Dre during that time was in no way mentally or spiritually healthy for him. Who better to talk about what is happening in hip-hop than Bow Wow? In the media, Bow Wow has been critical of a popular dance called the Dab, created by the rap group, Migos, from a song entitled, "Look at My Dab (B---h Dab)." Bow Wow took to social media to state the following: "The world [is] dabbing and they don't even understand or know what dab is. First of all, dab is a strong way to smoke marijuana, it's the purest form of marijuana. It's extremely strong, so the dance comes from when you smoking and you coughing, the first thing you do is [hits dab]." In his social media video post, he demonstrates the dance that requires you to quickly put your face in your inner elbow. Interestingly, the dance directly resembles coughing into your elbow, which is recommended by nurses in elementary school to prevent the spreading of germs when sneezing and coughing. While the rap group Migos denies Bow Wow's claims, the following lyrics of the song, "Look at My Dab (B---h Dab)," causes some to wonder if Bow Wow has a point:

Look at my dab, everybody sayin' dab

Trap n----s on the map, trap n----s like to dab
Trap n----s in the bowl, trap n----s on the stove
Trap n----s worldwide, play with the pie with no eyes
Dabbin' goin' in the dictionary, birds sangin' just
like Mary Mary
The bricks got wings like the tooth fairy, pinky
ring yellow canary...

The above lyrics summarize manufacturing and distributing drugs. Whether what Bow Wow is saying is true or not it is up to positive role models and youth leaders to translate to our youth that everything that looks good is not necessarily good. Oh, the great places our youth can go if they are not constantly attacked by Weapons of Mass Distraction and Oh, the destructive places our youth can go when they *are* attacked by Weapons of Mass Distraction.

Be Overprotective

I am concerned for the rappers who were hurt as children, never taught to cry, so they cry bullets and spit slurs in their music, all while lyrically assassinating the lives of many of today's youth by poisoning their dreams! It is vitally important for parents, teachers, and many youth leaders that need to understand that the youth, no matter their age, need our protection! Years ago, I met President Bush at a conference. The day he arrived, everyone was screaming his name like he was a rock star and wanted to take pictures with him, including me. Amid all of that, I noticed that his security guards, several of them, were diligently protecting him. They were ready to give their lives for the president. This was the most protection for one man that I have ever seen!

I believe our youth are valuable enough to be overprotected. I believe the talents, gifts, abilities, and purposes within each person on earth are worth going overboard to guard. Growing up in poverty, without my father who fathered about 20 children with several different women, I was raised with my twin brother, Howard Jean, and my little sister, Rosa Jean. Our single parent mother, Vanessa Jean, is one of America's most dynamic women in my opinion. Though Weapons of Mass Distraction were all around my neighborhood, my mother worked hard to ensure that they didn't get to us. With little to no money, she spent time investing in our minds instead of what was on our feet. She was constantly teased by her friends for being so strict on us and not letting us have the fancy things in life. They would tell her that she was too overprotective. Overprotection is not a sin!

My mother would tell us, "I care more about your self-worth than material things." We held on to these words when we were bullied or when we did not experience the type of "Christmas" most of our friends were experiencing. Every Christmas, we would wake up to her apologizing for not being able to get us what we wanted. Instead, we woke up to an annual home-cooked delicious breakfast feast on every Christmas morning. Cooking breakfast was her way of giving us the best of what one could provide. Our mother treated parenting like a mission and we didn't question her. As her children, we always felt like we were a part of something greater. Our mother made us feel that way! When people would bully me, I was able to handle those experiences because of what my mother instilled in me. She would tell us things like, "I'm supposed to feed you, clothe you, and take care of your basic needs. If I don't, I can go to jail. I want to put something in you and help you realize your self-worth." She didn't allow us to listen to the negative rap music on the radio because the content opposed what she was teaching and what we were learning in church.

Having been a former recording artist, my mother recognized the power of music. There were many times I would sneak to listen and record some of my favorite rappers as a kid and memorize them. I love music! However, when I grew older, I eventually realized that all my mother had said made sense, and I coupled that with my own learning. Today, my twin brother is a CEO and successful entrepreneur and my sister is an educator, great wife, singer and awesome mother. I became the principal of an elementary school, motivational speaker, author, pastor, and a community leader. All this because my mother was overprotective. I wasn't allowed to spend the night at everyone's house. I wasn't allowed to ride in cars with everyone, and I had minimal privacy during my training ground as a son in my mother's house. None of this was because my mother didn't trust me. However, it was because she did not trust the influences and potential distractions that could cause me to do something that was not in my character. She prayed with us, read the Bible with us, and made sure we were involved in our church and that we served in our community (i.e. picking up trash, cleaning yards for the elderly, etc.). My siblings and I were products of the old adage, "It takes a village to raise a child." My village was made up of my extraordinary uncles, my angelic grandparents, godparents, big cousins, church families and community elders. My mother orchestrated my village and worked in partnership with them to ensure I had the best God intended for me to have in order to become a man.

Like my mother did, we must teach the youth their value and how to respond to life. If there is no parent to do that, then we must seek people that can provide this type of support. There

Hayward R. Jean

are tremendous numbers of young people committing suicide because they do not know how to respond to the challenges of life, and they do not have a village keeping them on the right path.

In Chapter Three, I wrote about how I put on a costume in church. During my speaking, I decoded a lot the rap songs that were popular at the time. While many young people at that time were rocking to Soulja Boy, and doing the "Superman," there were speculations that the song had a deeper meaning, and the dance, spoke of something sexually explicit and degrading done against a female. When I shared this and other lyrical content that were secretly damaging to young kids, the response of parents and church was an eye opener to me that we, as a society, need to be more aware of what our children are listening to and watching. Church leaders and parents were crying and grabbing their children, apologizing to them, and repenting before God for not being watchful. Many of the young people even expressed that they did not want to allow themselves to be "played" again by the music they were playing.

Harmful Exposure

Sending children to their bedrooms is not always punishment anymore because in their bedrooms the world is at their fingertips if they have cell phones or computer devices. While there are pedophiles lurking the internet, Weapons of Mass Distraction are equally harmful to the youth. Some of the songs about sex, along with the provocative dance moves by many of today's popular artists are just as dangerous in nature as child molesters. This is in addition to the hundreds of rap videos with females dancing like strippers and young boys and girls in the videos with them. There are even videos of young girls, ages two and up, dancing like strippers on YouTube and parents cheering them on, because they saw their favorite artist doing it.

The Irony of Mainstream Hip-Hop Music

Artists who help create Weapons of Mass Distraction are covering up something that they are ashamed of which causes them to take on a personality and even a stage name that are not theirs and are very inappropriate for youth. The responses these artists often offer the media seem ironic considering they interview and rap about not having a father or mother while growing up.

One such response to the question "are you concerned about young people that listen and are influenced by your music?" was given in an interview on the O'Reilly Factor conducted in the fall of 2003, with rapper and rap mogul Cam'Ron and Damon Dash. Education expert, Salome Thomas-EL, also participated in their heated discussion about the topic of gangster rap music and its influence on youth. Mr. Thomas-EL is a national education expert and best-selling author of two books entitled, *I Choose to Stay: A Black Teacher Refuses to Desert the Inner City* and *The Immortality of Influence*. He was a teacher and principal with the Philadelphia School District and received national acclaim as a teacher and chess coach at Vaux Middle School, where his students have won world recognition as Eight-Time National Chess Champions. Mr. Thomas-EL was also a regular contributor on "The Dr. Oz Show." Mr. Thomas-EL uses his life to educate and empower young people. During the interview, Thomas-EL asked the following question to the rappers:

> … there are many young people who are affected by the lyrics, by the example of the videos. They talked about how Ludacris—many of them knew about

a video that Ludacris has where there's strippers and lap dances and those kinds of things, and these are 11, 12, and 13-year-old students who are very aware of what goes on. And I was just wondering what your thoughts were on whether you thought you really had an impact on the lives of young people and whether you thought it was negative or positive?

Cam'Ron's response was,

> At the end of the day, yes, you've got an influence on it, but so do movies. Like with me, I'm just an author. So what I do is I write what goes on in the ghetto. I'm not a liar. So what I tell you goes on in my album, that's what goes on in the streets of Harlem. Now, I'm like a reporter. When you look at the news, you don't get mad at the person reporting the news.

Thomas-EL further responds and explains to Cam'Ron with the following: "We're growing up in a fatherless society. A lot of our friends—your friends, my friends—didn't have a lot of supervision at home. Most of the time, they were at our homes. We had good parents. We had parents who didn't allow us to do or watch these kinds of things. I'm a critic of the movie industry also. I think that the kids are watching too much TV period. But my issue is that when you rap, you rap about what these children relate to because it's in their environment. You've already stated that they don't know your story because you're a CEO and I agree. But, see, you don't promote this and your company doesn't promote that. They promote the four-letter words" ("Is Gangsta Rap Music Hurting America's Children?", 2003).

15 years later, the influence of negative hip hop music is stronger than ever. Legendary rapper and one of the most influential artists in mainstream hip hop, Snoop Dogg, admits to his role in contributing to the negativity in an interview at the 2018 Essence Fest, while discussing his purpose for recording a gospel album. Interviewer, Steve Jones, moderated the panel that included gospel greats, Mary Mary and Marvin Sapp, along with Snoop Dogg. Jones asked Snoop "What is it about this timing now that caused you to do a faith-based project and why?" Snoop's response was "I just felt like the world that we living in right now, it's so much negativity, it's so much darkness, and I had a way with leading people to the darkness, so let me see if I can lead people to the light."

We Can Do This

There used to be a time when adults cared about saying certain things around youth. We made our children show respect when grown people were talking, but now our children are allowed to listen to anything adults say and are even allowed to join in. As adults, we are almost becoming accomplices to the kidnapping of our children's innocence. Young people are listening to music that contains information they should never have to know about.

I know there are other forms of entertainment that include artists with equally damaging content such as many of the movies, musical genres, and possibly even some compromising gospel artists. While I am very critical of the other forms of media, this is the force that has more of an impact on populations I see around me and in the news daily. Every year, I am apologizing to my students for the messages that are coming out of adults in the music industry. Some of my most painful experiences

69

are when I defend my female students from the sexual images portrayed by many of today's popular R&B and Hip-Hop female recording artists. Many of my girls and boys do not have proper adult supervision in their communities and this is the case around the world. Is the money so good that we would risk the mental, emotional, and even physical lives of our youth? What about how we value them? There is a song by Grammy-Winning Yolonda Adams that says,

> What about the children
> to ignore is so easy
> So many innocent children
> Will choose the wrong way
> So what about the children
> Remember when we were children?
> And if not for those who loved us
> And cared enough to show us
> Where would we be today? (Adams)

Our success is only as good as the success of our children. If our children are destroyed by Weapons of Mass Distraction, then our world will be destroyed by the same. Let's win our children. Let's fight for them, teach them, and train them in the way they should go!

We can do this!

Acknowledgements

Thank you, God, for choosing me to impact the youth and those who love them. This project is unto You!

To my dynamic wife, Starlette! Your encouragement was powerful during this writing process! I love you more than words can say!

Thank you, Micah, Malachi and Imani, for being dynamic children. I love being your dad.

Thank you, Mom, for teaching me the power of knowing my self-worth! Your life lessons are a tremendous part of the foundation for this project!

Thank you, Daddy! I am honored to be your grandson! You are a model of strength.

Thank you, Terry, for the awesome editing of my first project! You made the experience enjoyable, educational, and empowering!

Thank you, Greg, for your tremendous advice and expertise on the book cover! You are a genius!

Thank you to Apostle Wall, The Feast of the Lord family and the Call Me MISTER program. You were the first ones to hear this message. Thank you for providing for me a great training ground for purpose discovery and fulfillment.

Thank you, David Marshall, Jr. of *David Help!* Jordone Massey, Eddie Massey III, and William J. Wisniewski for your support in the 4th quarter of this project.

Works Referenced

"O, Let's Do It" by rapper, Waka Flocka Flame, Released April 14, 2009

"Live Fast, Die Young" by rapper, Rick Ross (feat. Kanye West), Released July 20, 2010

"Suicidal Thoughts" by late rapper, Biggie Smalls, Released September 13, 1994

"Biggie Smalls: Rap Man of the Moment" in the New York Times, December 18, 1994 by Toure

"Death Around the Corner" by late rapper, Tupac Shakur, Released March 14, 1995

"Nuthin'" by rapper Lecrae, released September 9, 2014

"It's Time to Empower the Mind" by Hayward Jean, Released 2009

"Married to the Money" by Trey Songz (feat. Chrisanity) Speaker Knockerz sample, Released May 21, 2015

The Mis-Education of the Negro by Carter G. Woodson, Publication date 1933

"Researcher cites negative influences of hip hop" by Kathy SaeNgian, former contributor for the Pittsburgh Post-Gazette, June 13, 2008

"Traumatized" by rapper Meek Mills, Released October 30, 2012

"Where Have You Been?" By rappers Jay-Z and Beanie Sigel, October 31, 2000

Oprah Talks to Jay-Z, The Exclusive O Interview, *O, The Oprah Magazine*, October 2009

U.S. Census Bureau's 2016 Current Population Survey Annual Social and Economic Supplement

National Center for Fathering, Fathering in America Poll

"Take Back the Music" by Dr. Carolyn West, January 2005 *Essence Magazine*

"Look at my Dab" by rap group, Migos, Released October 30, 2015

"Is Gangsta Rap Music Hurting America's Children?" The Impact Segment on the *O'Reilly Factor* with Education expert Salome Thomas-EL and rap moguls, Cam'Ron and Damon Dash, November 12, 2003

"What About the Children" by gospel artist, Yolonda Adams, Released October 1995

 **Speak Life**

Join the Movement!

Let's Connect!

Hayward R. Jean

Haywardjean.com

 HaywardJean

 @haywardrjean

 @haywardjean

 @hayward_jean

CPSIA information can be obtained
at www.ICGtesting.com
Printed in the USA
FFHW010857281019
55768664-61643FF

9 780692 043066